Hal•Leonard
pro Vocal®
BETTER THAN KARAOKE!

MAMMA MIA!™

ISBN 978-1-4234-3377-4

HAL•LEONARD®
CORPORATION

7777 W. BLUEMOUND RD. P.O. BOX 13819 MILWAUKEE, WI 53213

Visit Hal Leonard Online at
www.halleonard.com

Dancing Queen

Words and Music by Benny Andersson, Björn Ulvaeus and Stig Anderson

Intro-Chorus
Moderately

You can dance, _ you can jive, _____ hav - ing _____ the time of _____ your

life. _____ Ooh, _____ see that _ girl, _ watch that _ scene, _ dig - gin' the

danc - ing _____ queen. _____

Verse

Fri - day night _ and the lights are low, _____

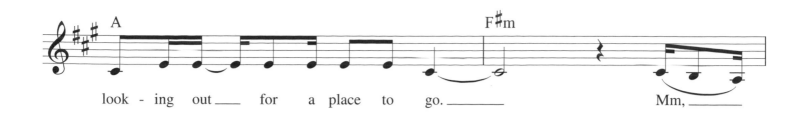

looking out ___ for a place to go. _____ Mm, _____

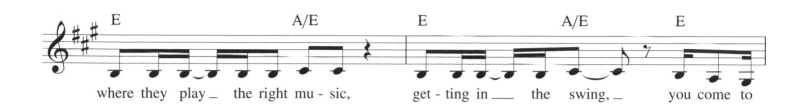

where they play ___ the right mu-sic, get-ting in ___ the swing, ___ you come to

look for a king. ____

Verse

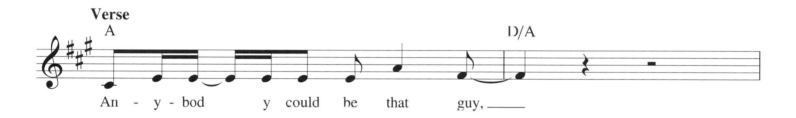

An - y - bod - y could be that guy, _____

night is young ___ and the mu-sic's high; _____

with a bit ___ of rock mu-sic ev - 'ry - thing ___ is fine. You're in the

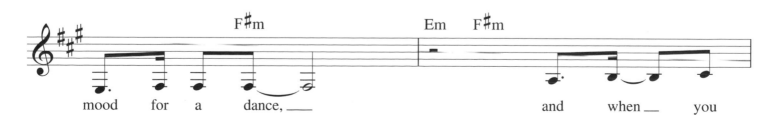

mood for a dance, ___ and when ___ you

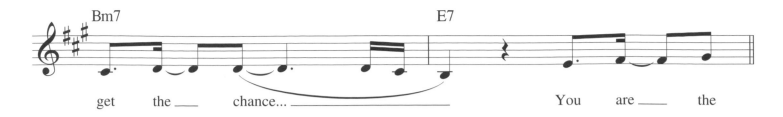

get the ___ chance... _____ You are ___ the

𝄋 Chorus

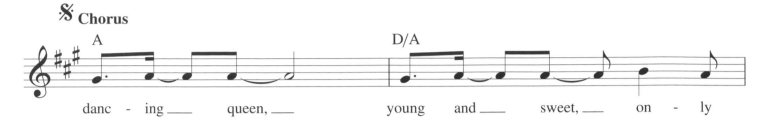

danc - ing ___ queen, ___ young and ___ sweet, ___ on - ly

sev - en - teen. ___ Danc - ing ___ queen, _

feel the __ beat __ from the tam - bou - rine, _ oh yeah. _____

You can dance, _ you can jive, ____ hav - ing __ the time of __ your

life. ___ Ooh, _____ see that _ girl, _ watch that _ scene, _ dig- gin' the

To Coda ⊕

danc - ing ___ queen. _____

Verse

You're a teas - er, you turn 'em on, _____

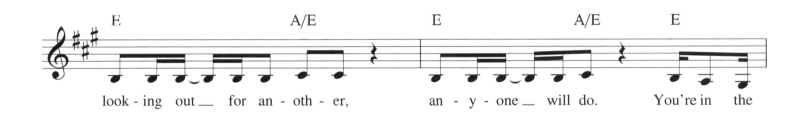

leave them burn - ing and then you're gone;

look - ing out __ for an - oth - er, an - y - one __ will do. You're in the

mood for a dance, _ and when __ you get the __ chance... _____

D.S. al Coda   ⊕ **Coda** **Outro**

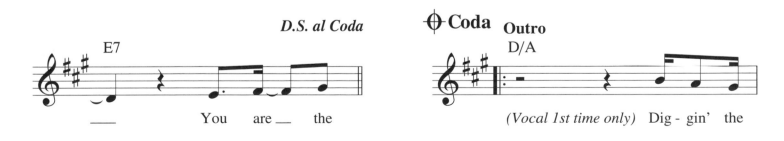

_____ You are __ the   *(Vocal 1st time only)* Dig - gin' the

danc - ing _____ queen. _____

Honey, Honey

Words and Music by Benny Andersson, Björn Ulvaeus and Stig Anderson

So stay on the ground, _ girl, you'd bet-ter not get _ too high. _

There's no oth-er place in this world _ where I'd rath - er _ be. _

Outro

Hon-ey, hon-ey, how _

_ you thrill _ me. Uh - huh. Hon-ey, hon-ey.

Begin Fade out

Hon-ey, hon-ey, near - ly kill _ me. Uh - huh. Hon-ey, hon-ey.

I'd heard a-bout you _ be - fore. _____ I

Fade out

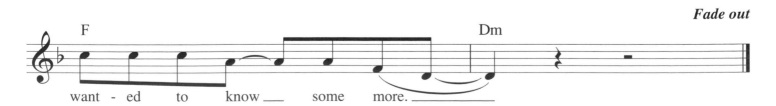

want - ed to know _ some more. _____

I Have a Dream

Words and Music by Benny Andersson and Björn Ulvaeus

Mamma Mia

Words and Music by Benny Andersson, Björn Ulvaeus and Stig Anderson

Intro
Moderately fast

Verse

I've been cheat-ed by you ___ since I don't ___ know when, ___
I've been an-gry and sad ___ a-bout things that you do. ___

so I've made up my mind ___ it must come to an end. ___
I can't count all the times ___ that I told you we're through. ___

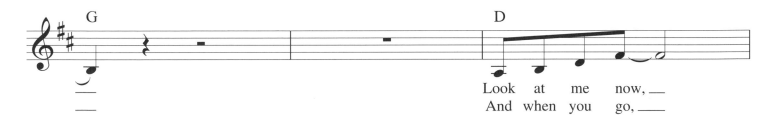

Look at me now, ___
And when you go, ___

will I ev-er learn? I don't know how, ___ but I sud-den-ly lose ___
when you slam the door, I think you know ___ that you won't be a-way ___

con - trol, _____ there's a fire __ with - in _____ my soul. __
too long. _____ You know _ that I'm not ____ that strong. _

Pre-Chorus

Just one look and I can hear a bell ring. __ One more

Chorus

look and I for - get ev -'ry - thing, __ oh, __ oh. __ Mam - ma mi - a,

herc I go a - gain, _ my, my, how __ can I re - sist ya

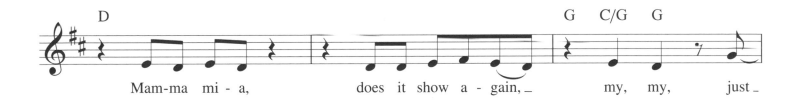

Mam - ma mi - a, does it show a - gain, _ my, my, just _

__ how much I missed ya? Yes, __ I've been bro - ken - heart - ed,

blue __ since the day __ we part - ed. Why, why did _

To Coda ⊕

__ I ev-er let you go? __ Mam-ma mi-a, now I real-ly know, __

my, my, I _____ can nev-er let you go. __ e-ven if I say, __

bye-bye, leave __ me now or nev - er. Mam-ma mi-a,

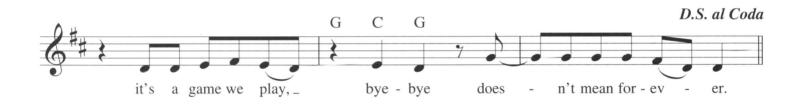

D.S. al Coda

it's a game we play, _ bye-bye does - n't mean for-ev - er.

⊕ **Coda**

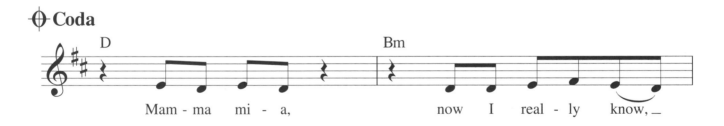

Mam-ma mi-a, now I real-ly know, __

Outro

my, my, I _____ can nev-er let you go. __

Repeat and fade

Slipping Through My Fingers

Words and Music by Benny Andersson and Björn Ulvaeus

Verse
Moderatley slow

School - bag in hand, __ she leaves __ home in the ear - ly morn - ing,

wav-ing good-bye with an ab - sent - mind - ed smile.

I watch her go __ with a surge of that well-known sad - ness,

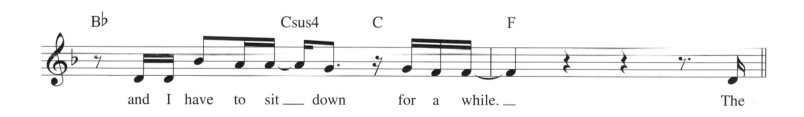

and I have to sit __ down for a while. __ The

Bridge

feel - ing that I'm los - ing her __ for - ev — er, and

with-out real - ly en - ter - ing ___ her world. ___   I'm

glad when - ev - er I ___ can share her laugh - ter, that fun - ny, lit - tle girl. ___

%
Chorus

___ Slip-ping through my fin-gers all ___ the time, ___ I try to cap-

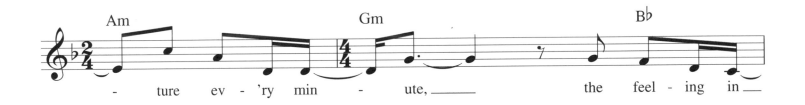

- ture ev - 'ry min - ute, ___ the feel - ing in ___

___ it. Slip - ping through my fin-gers all ___ the time. ___ Do I real-ly see what's in ___ her mind? ___

To Coda ⊕

___ Each time I think ___ I'm close to know - ing, ___ she keeps on

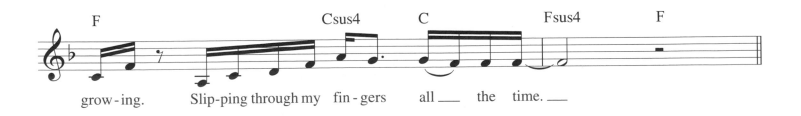

grow-ing. Slip-ping through my fin - gers all ___ the time. ___

Verse

Sleep in our eyes, _ her and me _ at the break - fast ta - ble.

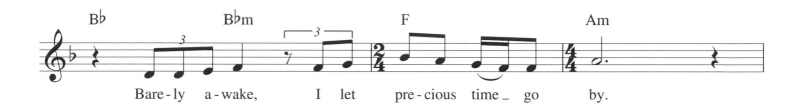

Bare - ly a - wake, I let pre - cious time _ go by.

Then when she's gone, _ there's that odd mel - an - chol - y feel - ing

and a sense _ of guilt _ I can't de - ny. What

Bridge

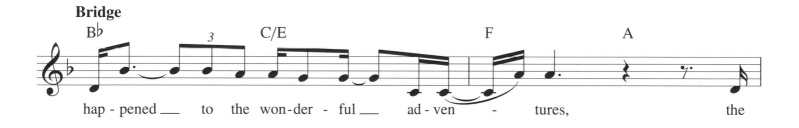

hap - pened _ to the won - der - ful _ ad - ven - tures, the

plac - es _ I had planned for us to go? _ Well, _ some of that we did; _ but most, we

did - n't, And why? I just don't know. _ Slip - ping through my

19

grow - ing.   Slip - ping through my fin - gers   all ___ the time. ___   Some -

Bridge

times   I   wish that   I _____ could freeze _   the   pic - ture   and

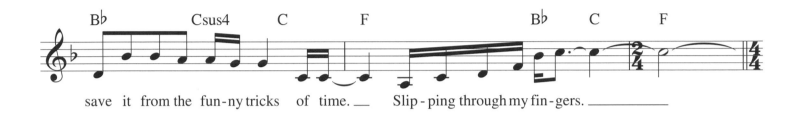

save   it from the fun-ny tricks   of time. __   Slip - ping through my fin - gers. _____

Interlude (Chorus)

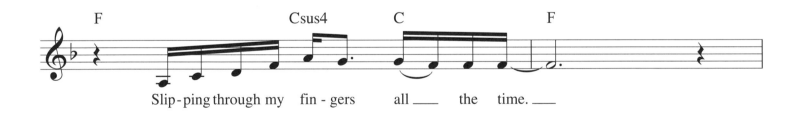

Slip - ping through my   fin - gers   all ___ the   time. ___

Outro

School - bag   in hand, _   she leaves home __   in   the ear - ly morn - ing,

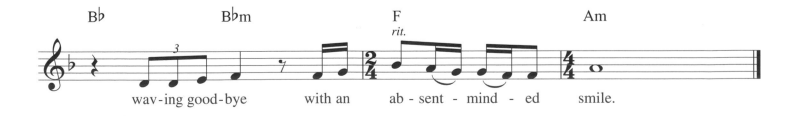

wav - ing good-bye   with an   ab - sent - mind - ed   smile.

20

Super Trouper

Words and Music by Benny Andersson and Björn Ulvaeus

Intro
Moderately

Su - per troup - er beams are gon-na blind _ me, but I ___ won't feel _

blue, ___ like I al - ways _ do, ___ 'cause

Interlude

some-where in the crowd there's _ you.

Verse

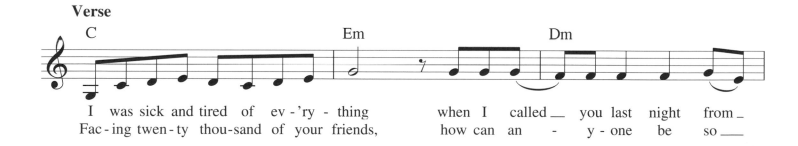

I was sick and tired of ev - 'ry - thing   when I called _ you last night from _
Fac - ing twen-ty thou-sand of your friends,   how can an - y - one be so ___

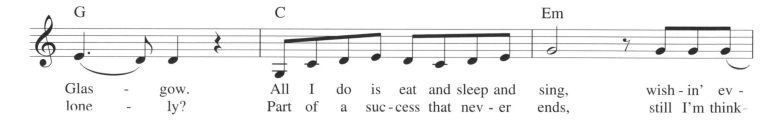

Glas - gow.   All I do is eat and sleep and sing,   wish - in' ev -
lone - ly?   Part of a suc - cess that nev - er ends,   still I'm think-

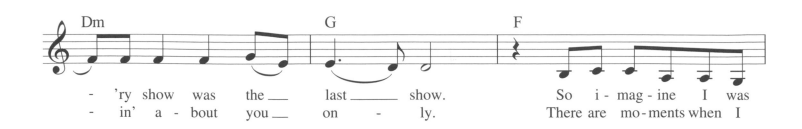

- 'ry show was the ___ last _____ show.   So i - mag - ine I was
- in' a - bout you ___ on - ly.   There are mo - ments when I

glad to hear you're com - ing.   Sud - den - ly I feel al - right.
think I'm go - in' cra - zy   and it's gon - na be al - right.

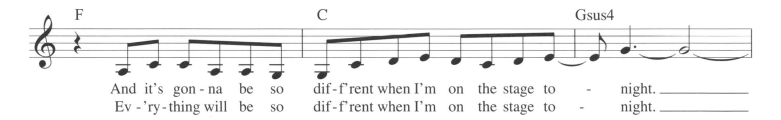

And it's gon - na be so dif - f'rent when I'm on the stage to - night. _____
Ev - 'ry - thing will be so dif - f'rent when I'm on the stage to - night. _____

Chorus

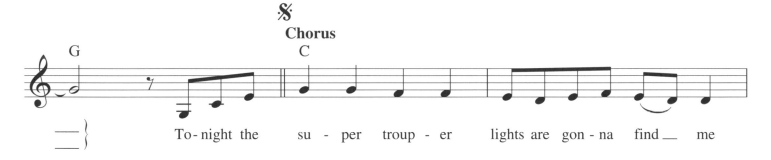

___ }   To - night the su - per troup - er lights are gon - na find ___ me

shin - in' ___ like the ___ sun,   smil - in', hav - in' ___

fun,   feel - in' like a num - ber one.   To - night the

su - per troup - er beams are gon - na blind _ me,   but I _____ won't feel ___

blue, like I al - ways __ do, 'cause

To Coda ⊕

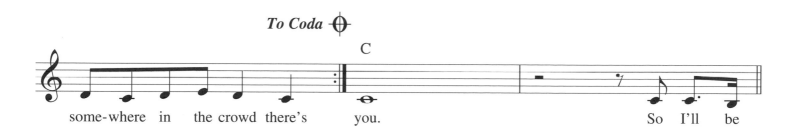

some-where in the crowd there's you. So I'll be

Bridge

there when you ar - rive. The sight of you will prove to me I'm still a-

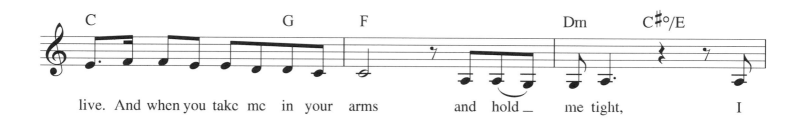

live. And when you take me in your arms and hold __ me tight, I

know it's gon - na mean so much to - night. _____ To-night the

⊕ **Coda**

Outro

you. Lights are gon-na find __ me shin - in' __ like the __ sun,

smil - in', hav - in' __ fun, feel-in' like a num - ber one.

Take a Chance on Me

Words and Music by Benny Andersson and Björn Ulvaeus

If you change your mind, ___ I'm the first in line, ___ hon-ey, I'm still free, ___

___ take a chance on me. ___ If you need me, let ___ me know; gon-na be a - round ___

___ if you got no place ___ to go when you're feel-ing down. ___

If you're all a - lone ___ when the pret-ty birds ___ have flown, hon-ey, I'm still free, ___

___ take a chance on me. ___ Gon-na do my ver - y best and it ain't no lie, ___

if you put me to ___ the test, if you let me try. ___ Take a

chance on me. _____ Take a chance on me. _____

Verse

We can go __ danc - ing, we can go __ walk - ing, __ as

long as we're __ to-geth - er. Lis - ten to __ some mu - sic,

may-be just __ talk - ing; __ you'd get to know __ me bet - ter. 'Cause you know I got

so much that I wan-na do, __ when I dream I'm a-lone with you, __ it's

mag - ic. __ You want me to leave it there, __ a-fraid of a love af-fair, __ but I

D.S. al Coda

think you know _ that I can't let go. __ If you change your mind, _

Chorus

I'm the first in line, ___ hon-ey, I'm still free, ___

take a chance on me. ___ If you need me, let ___

me know; gon-na be a - round ___ if you got no place ___

to go when you're feel-ing down. ___ If you're all a - lone ___

when the pret-ty birds ___ have flown, hon-ey, I'm still free, ___

take a chance on me. ___ Gon-na do my ver-

- y best, ba-by, can't you see? ___ If you put me to ___

Repeat and fade

the test, take a chance on me. ___ If you change your mind, ___

The Winner Takes It All

Words and Music by Benny Andersson and Björn Ulvaeus

Pro Vocal® Series
SONGBOOK & SOUND-ALIKE CD
SING GREAT SONGS WITH A PROFESSIONAL BAND

Whether you're a karaoke singer or an auditioning professional, the Pro Vocal® series is for you! Unlike most karaoke packs, each book in the Pro Vocal Series contains the lyrics, melody, and chord symbols for at least eight hit songs. The CD contains demos for listening, and separate backing tracks so you can sing along. The CD is playable on any CD player, but it is also enhanced so PC and Mac computer users can adjust the recording to any pitch without changing the tempo! Perfect for home rehearsal, parties, auditions, corporate events, and gigs without a backup band.

Visit Hal Leonard online at
www.halleonard.com

HAL•LEONARD®

7777 W. BLUEMOUND RD. P.O. BOX 13819 MILWAUKEE, WI 53213

Prices, contents, & availability subject to change without notice.

0113